DATE DUE	
MAY 0 7 1998	
SEP 1 4 1999	
AUG 1 6 2000	
FEB 2 1 2002	
JUN 2 6 2002	
DEC 1 3 2002	
MAR 3 0 2003	
AUG 2 3 2003	
MAY 1 9 2004	
APR 1 3 2005	
JUN 2 3 2005	
GAYLORD	PRINTED IN U.S.A.

"...and then

we'll get him!"

Richard Marek Publishers, New York

For permission to reprint cartoons, on pages listed, I gratefully acknowledge the following:

Audubon magazine, 10, 26, 65, 66; *Esquire,* 125; *Fantasy & Science Fiction,* 10, 13, 24, 50, 51, 56, 61, 66, 70, 72, 77 (both), 79 (both), 98, 99, 100, 123; *National Lampoon,* 40, 92 (both), 93 (both); *The New Yorker,* 19, 26, 82, 118; *Playboy,* 7, 12, 16, 22, 25, 33, 35, 38, 45, 48, 52, 54, 58, 64, 69, 71, 74, 78, 83, 85, 90, 94, 97, 102, 104, 109, 112, 115, 119, 121; Register and Tribune Syndicate, 8, 46, 53, 70, 81, 82, 98, 101, 106.

Library of Congress Cataloging in Publication Data

Wilson, Gahan.
". . . and then we'll get him!"

1. American wit and humor, Pictorial.
I. Title.
NC1429.W5785A4   1978   741.5'973   78-1312
ISBN 0-399-90003-9
ISBN 0-399-90014-4 pbk.

Book designed by Richard Celano

Printed in the United States of America
Second Impression

To Nancy

Other Books by Gahan Wilson

GAHAN WILSON'S GRAVEYARD MANNER
THE MAN IN THE CANNIBAL POT
I PAINT WHAT I SEE
PLAYBOY'S GAHAN WILSON
WEIRD WORLD OF GAHAN WILSON
GAHAN WILSON'S CRACKED COSMOS
FIRST WORLD FANTASY COLLECTION ANTHOLOGY

For Children

HARRY, THE FAT BEAR SPY
HARRY AND THE SEA SERPENT

"One day, when he's old and feeble, he'll be in a nostalgic
mood, and he'll come up here to see us again, and to reminisce—
and then we'll get him!"

". . . and you, of course, are the best man!"

"I think she heard us!"

"I've tried to make it as authentic as I could!"

"Then over there we put the pizzeria."

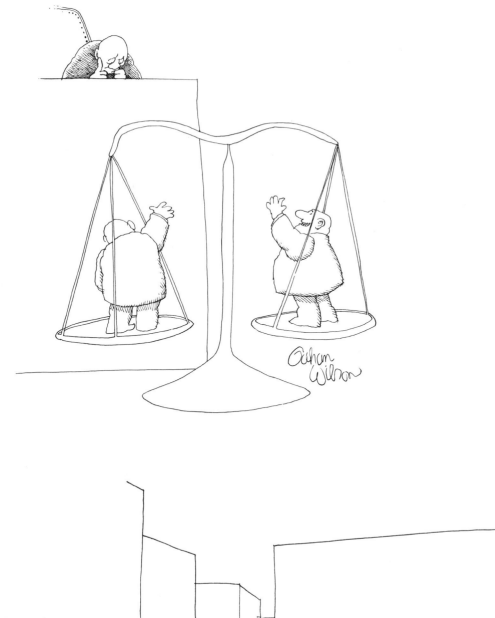

"Do you ever catch yourself wondering if all this
is only part of some crazy experiment?"

"Well, we found out what's been clogging up your drains!"

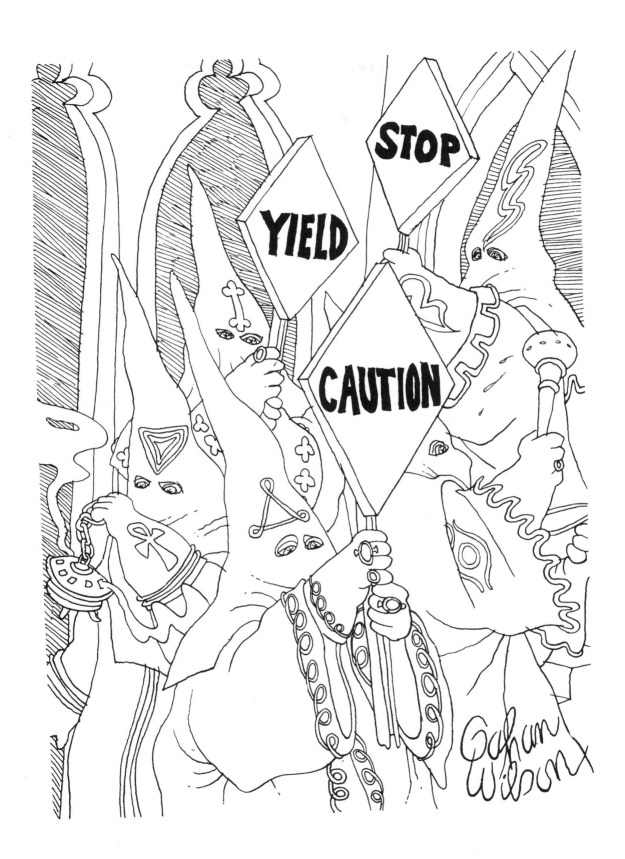

"I'll just take a half dozen
since they're super jumbo."

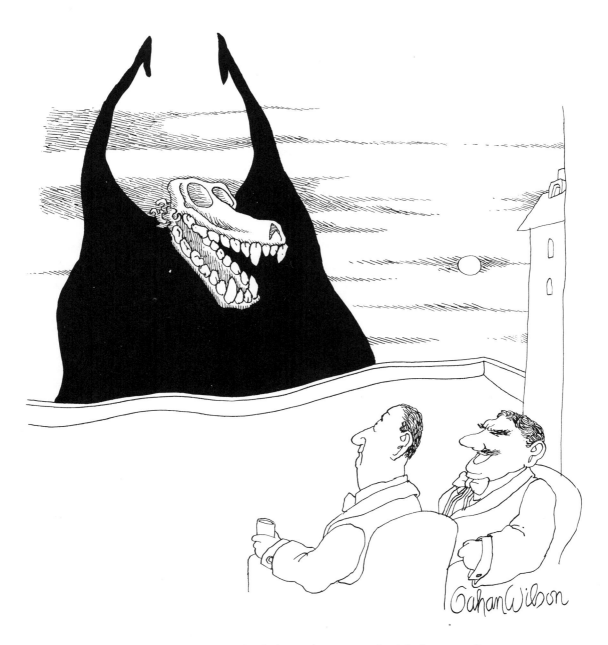

"There's an amusing little legend connected with that . . ."

"I'm sorry, young man, I just can't go through with this ceremony!"

"Cheap bastard!"

"Beat it, mac—this entourage is complete!"

"Something's wrong with Uncle Ted."

"Tell them I'm only human like everybody else."

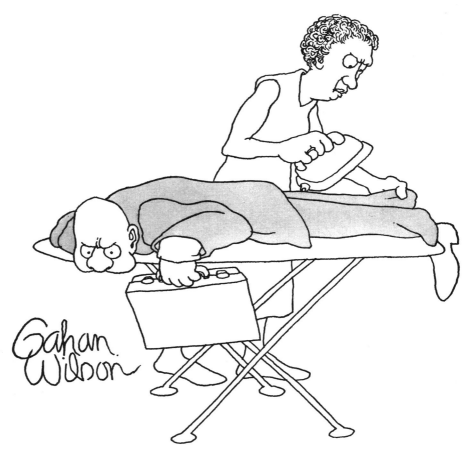

"Wait a minute.
There's another little wrinkly spot over here."

"I call it a club!"

"How the hell am I supposed to run a talk show
with guests like these?"

"What the hell *is* all this?"

"... but you're not interested in this job at all—
are you, Mr. Cosgrove!"

"First they guess wrong on Kohoutek, and now this!"

"Yes, Miller, I'm sparing no expense
in bringing our equipment here at Acme up to date."

"I've always *known* R.H. would be able to do that!"

"Look—who cares how much thyme you use?"

"... and get rid of that!"

"Really worked up quite an appetite last night,
eh, Mr. Blessing?"

"You mean you have survived the last seventeen years
on a diet of little green lizards?"

". . . but I'd forgotten that you've had him executed, haven't you?"

"For God's sake, man—do your part and bolt the stuff down!"

"Yes, these will do nicely."

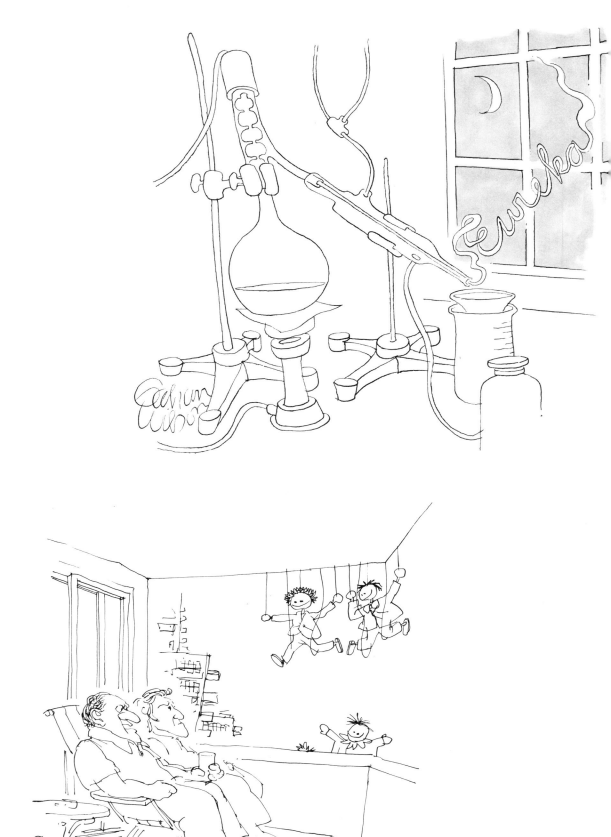

"Oh, God—now here go the people from downstairs!"

"On the other hand, if I'm dead, so what?"

"The view is over this way, you old fool!"

"Now if the F.D.A. doesn't tumble
to us, we'll make a bundle!"

"Third time I've spotted her this week!"

"When did you first become aware of this imagined 'plot
to get you,' Mr. Potter?"

"In your bare hands, as usual, Mr. Rodgers?"

"Of course, in life he was allergic to them."

"I'm sorry—where was I?"

"Say please."

"You'll be sorry you
did this,
Agnes!"

"Talk about your cut-rate operations . . ."

"Well, I'm sure *I* don't know him!"

"Think back, Margie! Did you go to a toy store, a
novelty shop—anything like that?"

"Me and my
big mouth!"

"I'm not going to shoot you, buddy—that would be too easy.
I'm going to let you live so you can stand trial!"

"Get me God again, Miss Parker."

"He hasn't been the same since George died."

"Then Mrs. Cratchit entered, smiling proudly, with the
pudding. Oh, a wonderful pudding! Shaped like a cannon-
ball, blazing in half-a-quartern of ignited brandy bedight
with Christmas holly stuck into the top, and stuffed full with
plums and sweetmeats and sodium diacetate and monoglyceride
and potassium bromate and aluminum phosphate and calcium
phosphate monobasic and chloromine T and aluminum potassium
sulfate and calcium propionate and sodium alginate and butylated
hydroxyanisole and . . ."

"... but I certainly appreciate your making the house call, doctor."

"When he's smiling, that means he's happy—right?"

"What are these funny black things
you've sewn onto your sleeves, Edwin?"

"Oh, yes—do come in!"

"All very well and good—but now we come to chart B."

"When will you accept it,
Hallahan? I *am* holier
than thou."

"OK, what the hell—I'll throw in Bulgaria."

"Here, puss, puss, puss!"

" . . . and around the corner ahead of you, to the left, is a picturesque, local ruffian laying in wait with a club . . ."

". . . but then I realized in order to make it work I'd have to invent a socket and God knows what else."

"I don't know, Harry, you used to be such great fun."

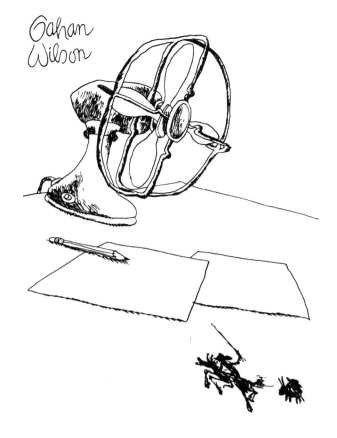

"I suppose it's got something to do with the operation
being held on Saint Valentine's day."

"My goodness, Mr. Merryweather, we certainly *did* make
a boo-boo with that prescription of yours!"

"T.G.I.F.!"

"To get to the main highway? Take the first left,
turn along the hill till you get to the Devil's mouth."

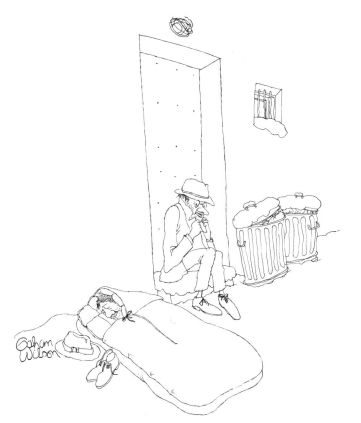

"Damn it, Fletcher—it's just not playing the game!"

"Keep chuckling. He has a way of suddenly
stepping back into the room."

"I think he's gone soft!"

"Well, there's not much here . . ."

"Gee—it's just like in the movies!"

"You're right—this scene *did* call for a stunt man!"

"You're spoiling it for the rest of us
on purpose, aren't you?"

"Take it from me, buddy—
at seventy-five score and ten it's a steal."

"Why, no, I can't say as how I ever noticed the resemblance."

"I'm afraid you got the wrong Martin Barker."

"You'd think a person who looked like Abraham Lincoln
would show a little self-respect!"

"Don't get it wrong, Bridget—the sacrifice of a white
rooster every third day at precisely high noon without fail!"

"Oh, shut up, Johnson. We'll go back to using puppies
the second they send us some more!"

"Harry—you're spoiling Thanksgiving for the children!"

"It was years before I realized
they don't really need me after a certain number of drinks."

"Oh, Irwin, I wish to God you'd get rid of that thing!"

"You're fired, Mysto!"

"Gee, I don't know; this is kind of depressing!"

"Where the hell's that kid got to?"

"I'll let you have one when you're not crazy."

"Harry, I really think you ought to go to the doctor."

"I'd say it's a pretty obvious case
of evolution taking a wrong turn."

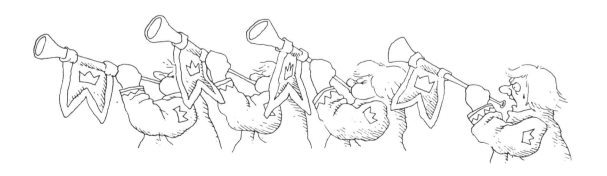

"Well—is he coming out or *isn't* he?"

"Tell me, Captain, how did you come to call your boat the *Revenge*?"

"Of course you realize this may be a difficult birth."

"Only mushrooms—no toadstools or footstools!"

"One small step for a znargh—a giant stride for znarghkind!"

"Young Brewster's really coming along, isn't he?"

"What's that, kid? I can't make out what you're trying to say."

"I'm over here, you fool!"

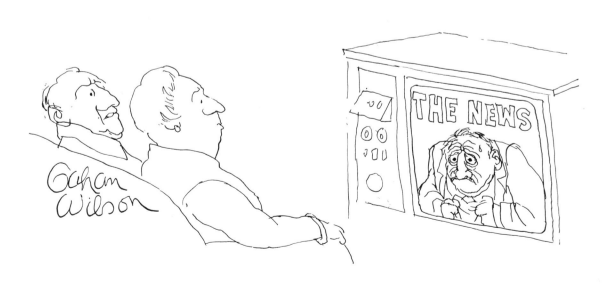

"My God—it must really be bad tonight!"

"Better get a replacement for Parker."

"Oh, stop bitching about it, will you? It's all
been over and done with for years?"

Gahan Wilson

"It's that bug that's been going around town."

"I'm sorry, Mr. Cheever, but there's absolutely nothing
in your warranty about the howler turning into a pumpkin."

"He can't stand the idea of no-fault insurance."

"That? Oh, that's a leftover
from more thoughtful days, I'm afraid!"

"Enough yin. More yang."

"General Electric beat him out on his death ray
and he's simply *furious*!"

"Seems like everybody's into that new fad diet!"

". . . and when it gets there I'm going to give it a little electric shock and
that will send it straight back up again!"

"Back where you belong, Rube."

"Don't let it push you around, Mrs. Harris!"

"So *that's* where it got to!"

"Dr. Kreuger—what are
you doing in my recurrent nightmare?"

"Floor, please."

"This is *not* going to help my Messianic complex, doctor."

"Of course he eats like a horse—
what in God's name did you expect?"

"I am sorry, ma'am, but this is really
very much out of my line."

"I'll talk! I'll TALK!"

"I'm afraid all we can do is operate
and hope they don't continue to spread!"

"Jesus Christ, Sergeant—what the hell kind of place
is this?"

"Alright, folks—let's give a great big welcome to little Miss Dynamite!"

"Didn't work out, eh?"

"Professor Zlata! you're just in time
to be the planet Neptune!"

"You any idea what these stains are, sir?"

"Now you've got to tilt it a little more to the back . . ."

"What the hell's that all about?"

"Ah, well—
back to
business."

"Let's get out of here—this place is driving me crazy!"
"Let's get out of here—this place is driving me crazy!"
"Let's get out of here—this place is driving me crazy!"
"Let's get out of here—this place is driving me crazy!"
"Let's get out of here—this place is driving me crazy!"

"The place has sure changed!"

"Oh, yeah, and forget that idea I had about hiring girl elves."

"You're not telling Mr. Bennett what he wants to hear!"

"You fiend—you could at least
let me have a little dignity!"

"I *knew* this would happen if those
damned conservationists had their way!"

"Er, what say we take that old pulse again, Mr. Ford?"

"Wow—that is some mount of Venus you have!"

"Mr. Thoreau is a very busy man!"

PARTY
FAVORS
AND
NOVELTIES

CLOSED
DUE TO
ANGST

"So *that's* where you got to!"

"Just what makes you think Charles' hobby
is getting out of hand, Mrs. Harding?"

"And to those of you who *did* contribute
to the church fund—our blessings."

"The patient is unaccountably depressed."

"The population explosion isn't bad enough, Handlesman,
you've got to dream up something like this!"

"By God—you're what I've needed
around here for years!"

"It's *deterrent*, Admiral, not detergent."

"See that, Stanley? *That*'s the kind of thing
I want you to avoid!"

". . . but enough of levity . . ."

"Yes, you are a square peg
in a round hole. Precisely."

"God knows it's cheap enough living here, but
it sure is depressing!"

"I'll have whatever you've got *à la financière*"

"Surprise!"

"I *told* you not to do that!"

"I can remember when that sort of thing
meant a lot to me!"

"We may already be too late, Mr. Parker."

"Good heavens—this must mean
we've practically finished him off!"

"All this fuss and bother just because
of a damned heart attack!"

"Remember when we first started coming out here, Sweetie?"

"Come on, folks—let's see if we can't bring him back
for just one more commandment!"

"Here comes that Wilson boy—all alone as usual."